WINNING WINDOWS

Decorating Made Easy

WINNING WINDOWS

Judy Sheridan, ASID

Park Lane Press
New York • Avenel, New Jersey

OTHER BOOKS BY
JUDY SHERIDAN

Instant Decor

Accessorizing Style

Perfect Picture Hanging

Copyright © 1996 by Judy Sheridan

This 1996 edition is published by Park Lane Press, distributed by
Random House Value Publishing, Inc.,
40 Engelhard Avenue, Avenel, New Jersey 07001.

Random House
New York • Toronto • London • Sydney • Auckland
Printed and bound in Singapore

Library of Congress Cataloging-in-Publication Data

Sheridan, Judy.
Winning windows / Judy Sheridan.
p. cm.
ISBN 0-517-20065-1
1. Drapery in interior decoration. I. Title.
NK2115.5.D73S5 1994
747' .5--dc20   94-11872
CIP

8 7 6 5 4 3 2 1

Credits:
Photography by David Regen
Design by Karine Bielefeld

TABLE OF CONTENTS

*W*hen I look at an interior in which the windows are without any sort of window treatment, I think of a woman who is all dressed up for an evening out and doesn't put on any jewelry. Something is not quite right—the look is unfinished.

Of course, there are those windows—usually large, with strong architectural styling such as one finds in a Palladian window—that look absolutely fine on their own. Special windows of this nature can be a dynamic element in the inherent style of a room. However, the percentage of us who have dwellings with such strong architectural endowments are, unfortunately, few.

Let's face it, most of us have windows, whether they be vintage or modern, that lack any significant style. We try to disguise the weaker aspects of a window with a window treatment. This, then, adds an element of design to the room interior. In fact, you can 'make' a room by what you choose to do with the windows. You can cover flaws, improve imperfect proportions, set a style or create a mood simply by how you dress your windows.

Think of the tremendous tool we have then, in the styling of a window. It's not unusual for a window treatment to be the major ingredient in a successfully decorated interior. To insure that the window treatment is also a success, we must step back and look at what is involved in good window design. We must begin at the beginning and look at the window itself.

When designing a window treatment, almost every window presents a challenge. All too often people are unable to come up with a design that will work within the specific physical constraints imposed by the window itself. Add how people would like their windows to look, and how they want them to physically function, and it is easy to see why designing a window treatment can be a challenge.

This book is written to keep you from becoming discouraged. First, by lessening, if not eliminating, your sense of frustration. Secondly, by enabling you to take all of the parts that make up the design of a window and see that a design is possible. And, finally, to envision that design and have it executed.

We've all seen photographs of lovely window treatments. Yet, try to duplicate an identical treatment on your window, and it usually doesn't work. Why is that? In order to understand the final design of a window treatment, you must also understand the thinking that preceded the design and then produced it.

I can think of no better way to illustrate this then to take real windows and their design solutions (let's call them "case studies"), and detail the various components that went into the thinking which resulted in the solution. For each example, I will first review the room and window itself. Then I'll explain the thinking process that ultimately resulted in the window treatment design.

To put this on as professional a level as possible, I have included the drawings that were made for each case study. A drawing, called the Window Wall Elevation, is provided for each window. It is the best way to see clearly what is happening with a window. Also included is the drawing of the final window design. Of course, these case studies would not be complete without a photograph of the actual window treatment as it was installed. The aim of this book is to show you how to approach window design, how to organize your thinking, how to develop designs, and, most important of all, how to gain the confidence to get it done and installed.

I. Styling Solutions for Heating/Cooling Units

Compatibility is the clue to designs that disguise unsightly mechanical equipment.

❧ CASE STUDY 1 ☙

The most common problem that I encounter with designing window treatments today is the bulky mechanical unit under the window. Usually centered on the wall, the unit can be an air conditioner, a radiator or a combination of a heating/cooling system. How is this situation best handled? In several ways, actually. I will present three good solutions to this type of problem.

— Solution One —
Visual Camouflage

In a Bedroom the use of a strongly styled table desk diverts the eye from the HVAC unit underneath the window.

The first solution is the simplest, as it only requires moving a piece of furniture that you may already own. If the top of the unit in question is between 24" (61cm) and 31" (79cm) from the floor, and is located underneath the window sill, place a piece of furniture in front of it. The objective is to have a piece of furniture that is close in measurement to the height of the window sill, and about as wide or wider than the offending unit in the wall. Keep it a few inches away from the wall so that it won't affect the air flow. When you do this, you visually distract the eye.

Facing Page: The finished window treatment with furniture that effectively disguises the heating/cooling unit.

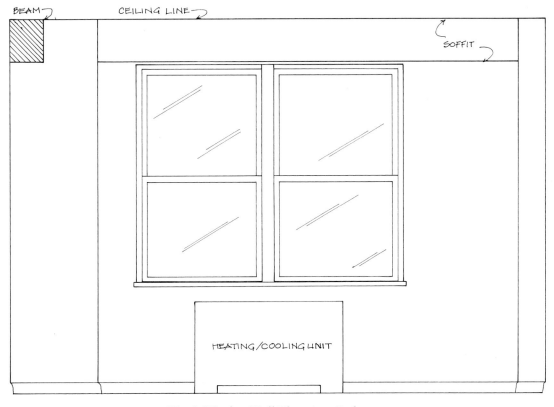

Fig. 1. Window Wall Elevation, Bedroom.

Instead of seeing the unattractive mechanism, the eye focuses on the more attractive object placed in front. For the best result, your piece of furniture should be

—*Tip*—

To truly camouflage the air conditioning/heating unit, paint or paper it to match your walls.

bigger than the unit in the wall, and that way you completely hide what's behind it.

The more attractive the piece of furniture, the more lovely the window elevation becomes when the window treatment is finished. The piece of furniture could be any of the following suggestions, bearing in mind that a factor in this decision will be the side-to-side measurement of the unit, as well as the height of your window sill:

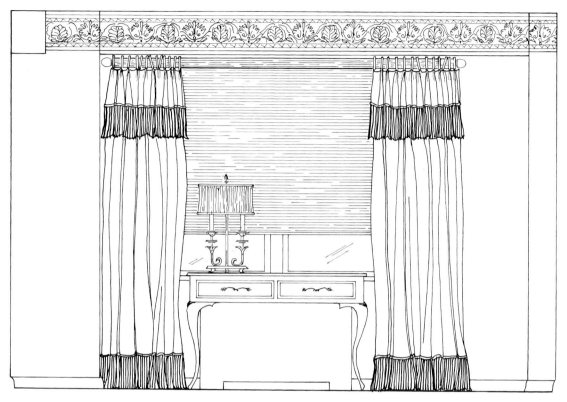

Fig. 2. Window treatment of stationary panels on a fluted wood pole with matching wood rings; the panels are trimmed with a very long bullion fringe.

❀ *a table desk*

❀ *a desk*

❀ *a credenza or sideboard*

❀ *a loveseat*

❀ *a lamp table flanked by 2 chairs*

❀ *a sofa*

❀ *a sofa table*

❀ *an interesting bench*

Any of these furniture types would be handsome silhouetted in front of a dressed window.

— Solution Two —
Drapery Concealment

A combination of curtains and furniture keeps a heating unit operating efficiently, but out of sight.

A second way to handle the problem of an unsightly mechanical piece of equipment in the window wall is to use floor length curtains to block it visually. Before selecting this solution, you will need to examine

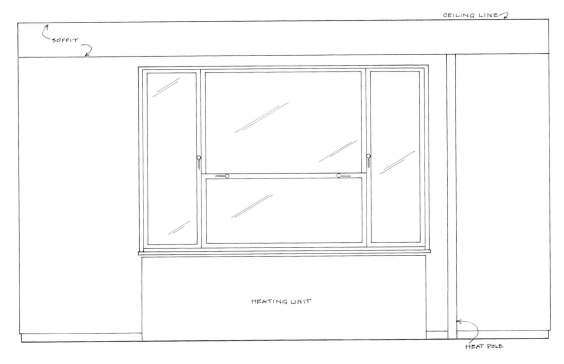

Fig. 3. Window Wall Elevation, Living Room.

the heating and/or cooling needs for the room. We will use a Bedroom for this example, since a bedroom usually requires more flexibility in the way the room temperature is controlled based on the daily habits and needs of the occupants. Whether privacy/visibility is a factor, whether it is to be light-proof or light-filled, cool or warm, the bedroom is a place where comfort is the priority.

For the purpose of air circulation, floor length curtains or draperies must be able to be opened and closed. Therefore, they need to be on a track—motorized or manually operated, or pulled by hand as in the case of draperies on a pole with rings.

At times when the curtains are opened for circulation or light, you may also want to provide additional covering on the window itself, either for reasons of privacy or because of an unattractive view. The best

Fig. 4. Window treatment of stationary drapery panels and upholstered cornice; floor length casement curtains are on a traverse rod.

choice for this would be a shade in a material that will meet your privacy/light requirements. Some aspects to consider are:

1. How visible do you want to be with the lights on at night?

2. Does it matter if you're visible during the daytime ?

3. When you wake up in the morning, does light bother you?

4. Do you want as much light in the room as possible during the day? If you're rarely home during the day, it probably won't matter very much.

5. Is the view out the window very attractive or best covered up?

6. Do you prefer having the windows open at night?

Overleaf: The casement curtains are completely hidden, stacked behind the drapery panels, revealing the heating unit behind the loveseat.

Determine when you will want to have the curtains fully or partially open:

    a. most of the time

    b. only at night

    c. only for air circulation

Or will you usually plan to have them closed:

    a. mostly for thermal protection

    b. only at night

    c. because this is the way the room looks best

These considerations will dictate the style of the treatment and types of fabric you will use. (For further information on fabric types and their uses, refer to the chart on page 91.) If the view isn't great and you definitely want privacy, then you would certainly choose a heavier fabric for the curtains than, for example, someone who wants to take advantage of the light. In the photograph on page 67, the fabric selected for the 'sheer' or casement curtains was sheer to maximize the available light, but was used in maximum fullness to cut down on the unattractive view outside.

Even if you think you will be opening and closing the curtains a good deal of the time, it might not be necessary to also have draw draperies. You can still have the look of draw draperies by using a pair of stationary hanging panels instead. These are drapery panels installed on either side of a window that give the same appearance as draw draperies.

A close-up of the double-layered trim: two different trims sewn together and used as one.

Stationary panels are designed to look as if they are on a traverse rod and could draw, but as the name implies, they are 'stationary' and don't move. In a situation where there is no need to have the draperies draw, don't hesitate to use stationary panels since they require less fabric and labor, and will save you money—always an important consideration. Stationary panels also provide a convenient cover for casement curtains when they are in the open position. Casement, glass or sheers, by the way, are different words used to describe the curtains that are always installed closest to the glass in a window or door.

To illustrate: let's say the first layer in your drapery treatment is the stationary panels. Immediately behind them, closer to the window, is a pair of casement curtains that you plan to keep open most of the time. When open and drawn to either side of the window, the drapery panels partially or completely conceal the casement curtains. Even with the glass area completely exposed, you maintain the look of a full-time drapery treatment. This results in a very finished look when combined with a pretty valance or upholstered cornice.

— Solution Three — Cabinetry Enclosure

A simple, pared-down approach for both the window and the mechanical equipment allows for a full range of cabinetry styles.

As you'll see, the next solution is more involved, but the end result is considerably more substantial. The idea is to enclose the entire section below the window sill with cabinetry, incorporating the heater or cooling unit. Generally speaking, the cabinetry should start at the level of the window sill and extend to the floor. Extend it from wall to wall, or from column to column—if there are columns at the corners of your window wall.

The top should be designed to include an opening for access to the controls on the unit, and a vent grill that is the means by which the heat or the cooled air circulates. Frequently the two are incorporated as a one-piece grill which lifts out of the top. There should be a removable separate

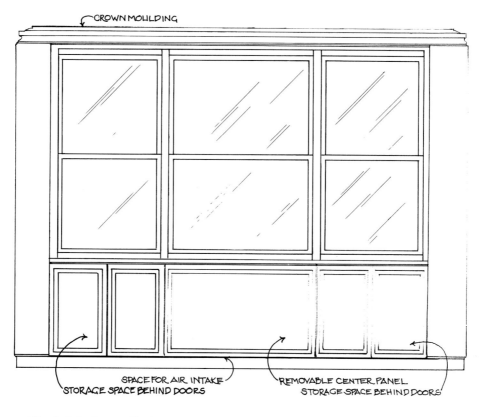

Fig. 5. Window Wall Elevation with built-in cabinetry enclosing the HVAC unit below the window.

panel in the front, the width of the unit, so that one has access to the unit for cleaning or for repairs. There needs to be space at the floor, about 3" (8cm), left open for room air to be pulled up into the unit. This is important, as neither warm nor cool air will circulate without this updraft from below. Then, whatever space remains on either side of this center section can be used for additional storage, if you choose.

This type of cabinetry can be made to take a wood finish, to look like wood paneling; it can be made in a "ready-to-paint" finish, then painted along with the rest of the room; or it can be finished in a plastic laminate.

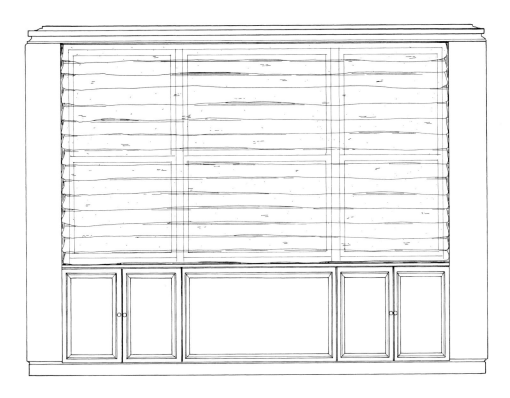

Fig. 6. Very much in keeping with the cabinetry style below it, a classic fabric shade is used on the window: unlined, sheer fabric with soft, unpressed pleats.

The advantages of building cabinetry under your window are:

1. having a very finished, professional looking window

2. being able to use a shade for the covering on the window (which by itself creates a very finished look)

3. eliminating the need for a more elaborate window treatment

4. creating that unmistakable air of quality that finely detailed cabinetry has

5. providing additional storage—the kind that is so useful to house stereo speakers

To insure a well built, soundly constructed installation, a woodworking or cabinetry shop should be consulted. Of course, if you have someone in your household who can produce a finished piece of cabinetry, I suggest you sign them up right away.

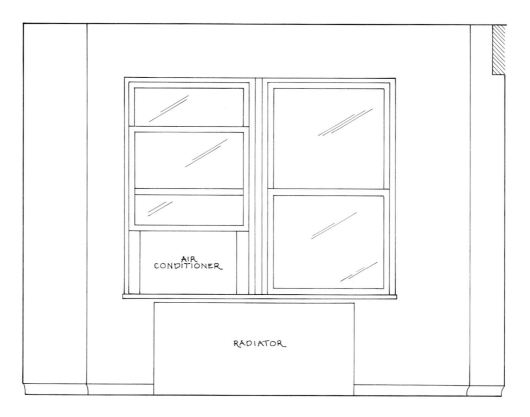

AIR
CONDITIONER

RADIATOR

Fig. 7. Window Wall Elevation, Bedroom.

In my view, this is the best solution for camouflaging such equipment because it keeps the mechanics of the heating and/or cooling system out of sight (worth almost anything in my estimation) and gives the entire window wall an architectural elegance which, by the way, does wonders for contemporary styles of housing construction.

CASE STUDY 2

Bedroom

To maintain an even level of comfort, sheer curtains provide various ways to access the air conditioner, fresh air or the radiator.

In the design world there is a type of a project known as 'carte blanche'. It means a client hires you to do the whole job, leaving you to make most or all of the decisions. This was the case here—I was working for a woman who wanted a total change, from top to bottom, in her Bedroom. She entrusted me to make most of the decisions.

Room and Window Review

1. A smallish Bedroom in an apartment, the primary window faces South and looks across a courtyard directly into other apartment windows.

2. No window trim, no mouldings in the apartment...typical of the era in which this building was built, the mid-sixties.

3. The double window, of thermal pane construction and recently installed,

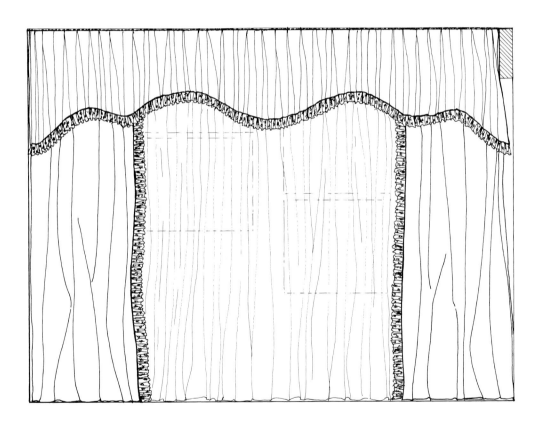

Fig. 8. A valance, stationary drapery panels, and casement curtain are combined to camouflage the air conditioner and radiator.

consists of two double-hung window units.

4. There is a second, single window in the Dressing Room, but I am to treat this as a separate issue. (See Case Study 8, page 77.)

5. The ceiling height is 8'-1"(2.46m) and there is a radiator set into the wall under the window sill.

6. A room-size air conditioner is located in the Left window.

Client Requests

1. As a working professional, the client seems to take change in her stride. She's not sure what she wants, she just knows that she wants a major change in the way her room looks.

2. She confides that she has been thinking about yellow all summer... but she is not sure that means a yellow bedroom.

3. She wants more coverage on the windows than she has had in the past. She is no longer interested in 'the view' or having light.

4. The room is normally quite warm, and she rarely turns on the radiator. Conversely, in the summer months, she doesn't use the air conditioner very much; she prefers to use an oscillating fan, except on the warmest nights.

5. She agrees with my assessment that the window treatment should be the dominant element in the room.

Design Development

Since I was going to approach the window as the focal point in the bedroom, I felt that the real excitement was going to come from an outstanding fabric or group of fabrics. Therefore, the 'design challenge' would be how I put the fabrics together. The more I thought about this approach the more it made sense.

—*Tip*—

An easy approach to decorating a Bedroom is to think of it as a fabric story. Let the fabric do the decorating. Put fabric on walls, windows, bed and furniture.

I saw the window treatment as consisting of a valance (probably a shaped valance) with drapery panels and a casement curtain— from wall to wall and from floor to ceiling. And I kept thinking I wanted something bold and gutsy.

The undulating bottom edge of the valance trimmed with a shirred ruffle in a jaguar pattern.

An unusual mix of stylized and natural patterns: stripes, jaguar, banana leaves and wrought iron gate.

A compelling window treatment; the shadow of the air conditioner barely perceptible behind the casement curtains on the Left.

Fabric and Color Choices

I wanted to find something unusual for this client. So I located a fabric firm that specializes in contemporary fabric designs. I asked if there were any directions in style, patterns, color or fibers that would give my client the big change she wanted. The response to my questions elicited the following information:

a. the new direction for home design fabrics is subjects that have to do with nature

—Tip—

So much of design is not a fool-the-eye exercise, but rather a distract-the-eye technique.

b. natural fibers…also very popular

c. as to directions in color, the answer, unexpectedly, is yellow! Now isn't that interesting.

The yellow color family seemed like a natural choice. There were so many irresistible fabrics. When I imagined the places I could use them, the walls seemed like a good place to start. They needed something. Why not use a fabric and upholster them?

Savoring the possibilities, I decided that the design for the room would be based on fabrics, using two key, large-scale patterns that would set the mood and determine the feel of the room:

* *one on the walls*
* *one for the draperies and valance.*

The concept of natural fibers was very appealing. A natural fiber like cotton for the fabrics would lend a softer, less formal, more inviting quality to the room. I knew I was taking a risk with these bold and colorful patterns, but I felt it would work in the end. Nevertheless, I kept wondering how the client would feel.

Solution

The more I thought about the window design the more my ideas had evolved about how it would look. I now wanted to use an undulating shaped edge for the valance. I thought this would detract from the rather box-like proportions of the room. When I first looked at fabrics, I responded most to a fabulous jaguar printed cotton. I wanted to do the whole room in it, even using it on the walls. After some serious thinking, I realized that over time it would not be an easy fabric for the client to live with.

Then I remembered an unusual fabric— a large open pattern on a muted yellow ground— that would be spectacular on the walls. But I still wanted to use the jaguar print. It was so alive. Why not use it to trim the draperies, both at the window and at the bed, on the headboard and for the tailored dust skirt? It would certainly make a statement, both subtle and specific.

The 'nature' theme had taken a hold of me. The primary fabric for the window treatment was a bold colorful pattern of banana leaves. Together with the jaguar print, it was breathtaking.

Special Note: One of the fundamental elements in the designer's character is the gravitational pull towards new, unusual, or different things. Many people have the opposite problem. If you find you resist trying anything but the 'tried and true', and if you are dissatisfied with the appearance of your surroundings, then I'm here to tell you that it's time to branch out!

A sedate finishing touch is the application of a wide band of the jaguar print to the hem of the bedspread.

EXPANSION EXERCISE

To help you flex your artistic wings and challenge your current comfort level, I want you to take the following "expansion exercise." It is to be taken seriously, but have some fun doing it.

1. Go to a store (housewares, home furnishings, accessories). Try selecting one thing for your home, it doesn't matter what it is (it can even be a yard of fabric), as long as it is appropriate for your interior.

2. BUT—your selection must be something you've never seen before, or something that you've seen before but have not considered purchasing, or something in a color you wouldn't dream of choosing. The item must prompt some resistance on your part, or the test won't work. However, it must also make sense for your interior.

3. Force yourself to buy it! Take it home and see how it feels. <u>Pretend you're the designer.</u> Look at it objectively.

4. Ignore all comments and responses from others. Pay attention only to your inner response.

5. Be dispassionate. Your reaction might surprise you.

6a. You may hate it. If you do, return it. Start over again with something else.

6b. Or you may think the item has possibilities. If so, it probably does.

7. Now ask yourself: Does the object seem "right" in your space, from the standpoint of
      a.)scale
      b.)proportion
      c.)color and
      d.)appropriateness?
   If you feel you can answer 'yes' to a., b., c., and d., then chances are you have something you should consider keeping.

8. As you evaluate the item objectively, is your feeling about it changing?

As you can see, this is not a pass/fail test—there is no scoring. What it is designed to do, however, is increase your awareness and expand your receptivity to new, different, and unexpected ideas.

Returning to our case study: I worked out the ventilation concerns in the following manner.

A traverse rod was used for the casement curtains. This allows the curtains to be opened for vacuuming or washing the windows. Then tie backs were provided: one on the Right window to pull the curtain back when the window is open for fresh air, another tie back, higher up on the Left, to pull that curtain back when the air conditioner is needed. Also, an opaque pleated shade was added to the window, behind the casements, so that the client would have full control over her privacy.

No doubt you're curious about how the client responded to this lively group of fabrics. Well, she absolutely loved the departure from the 'expected' that I offered her. This "carte blanche" project worked out very well—for both of us. ⚘

II. Designs for Window and Door Combinations

---❧---

Different combinations of sliding doors and windows generate outstanding window treatments.

CASE STUDY 3

Living Room

A window and sliding door combination designed to bring balance and drama to a room of significant proportions.

Here, I was asked by a client to organize a furniture plan for her large Living Room, and to design the window coverings, which she felt needed a professional hand. The room in question was quite handsome, sunny, and in spite of its size, inviting.

Room and Window Review

1. A very large Living Room in an old spacious house, with two newly installed French doors on one wall at the end of the room.

2. Immediately adjacent to this wall is one of the original windows. Very different in scale and style from the French doors. The sill is quite high, and so is the top of the window, which is close to the ceiling.

3. The French doors face South, and open out, onto a terrace. The terrace is used in the summer for entertaining; the doors are used as entrance doors the year round.

4. Overall ceiling height is 9'-1"(2.77m), which includes a nice-looking crown moulding, 3"(8cm) high.

5. If possible, the clients would like to retain the view from the East window.

6. The feeling of the room is slightly formal, probably because of its large proportions and an enormous rug

on the floor which has an overall trellis pattern and floral border in magnificent colors of pinky reds, fuschia and lavender.

Client Requests

1. This is a room that will be primarily used for entertaining. A formal window treatment is something that they feel they could relate to at this point in their lives.

2. Apparently, they have inherited the large rug, so the colors are not really 'theirs'. But, they seem happy enough with the colors to let me build the window treatment fabrics around them. So I will definitely incorporate the rug into our plans.

Design Development

Frequently, the real problems in designing a window treatment for a specific location do not become apparent until the window elevation has been drawn.

Such was the case here. Standing in the room and looking toward the French doors, I felt such a sense of space. It seemed that designing a large billowy window treatment would be easy to do and would create just the right feeling. But the wall elevations told a different story. They

revealed elements about the relationship between the window and the doors that I could not ignore. They were:

1. the tops of the window and the doors were at noticeably different levels;

2. the sill height seemed more exaggeratedly high than I remembered, especially with regard to the doors

3. the window and the Left door were each much closer to the corner than it seemed when I was in the room

4. the differences in proportion between window and doors were major.

I was tempted to use a pole with rings. But how could I keep three poles all at one level, with the different spacing above the window and doors? Either the pole at the window would be over the glass area, or the poles on the doors would be so high that a large expanse of wall would show.

Swags presented the same type of problem, as did valances. I was running through the repertoire of window dressing without much luck. Clearly, the solution for this situation was going to take some research. But, the valance idea seemed to give me a clue.

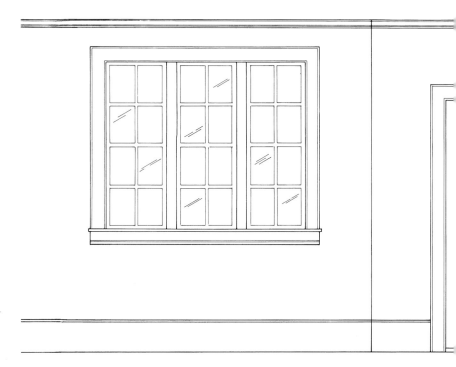

Fig. 9. Window Wall and French Door Wall Elevation, Living Room.

Fig. 10. A shaped cornice, stationary drapery panels and casement curtains on a traverse rod for both the window and French doors.

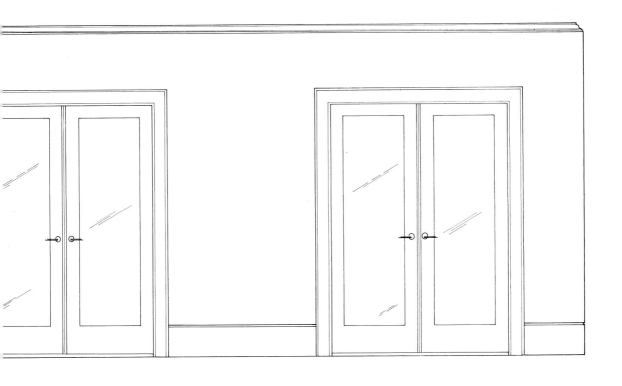

Next I focused on the crown moulding. Should it be covered, incorporated into the valance design or should I let it show? When I decided to cover it up and take the valance to the ceiling, the design started to come together.

By doing that—taking the valance to the ceiling—the drapery treatment became full height. As a result it enhanced the large proportions of the space, giving the room a better balance. In this one step, the direction the design would take was established.

Through a process of elimination, I settled on a shaped bottom for the styling of the valance. I would emphasize the shape of the valance edge with a strong use of trim.

At the last minute, I decided to include a pair of floor length casement curtains, installed on traverse rods, on each of the openings. This would create a balanced symmetry in the design and aid in controlling the sunlight coming through the French doors, even though it meant partially losing the view out the window.

The trims, which I planned to use on the edges of the valance and draperies, would bring the whole design into focus.

Fabric and Color Choices

I was curious to see how the sample fabrics would look when placed, alongside the rug with its delightful range of colors.

Special Note: Never select fabrics without checking the colors in daylight, as well as in the room's nighttime lighting. If there are substantial differences in the way the fabrics look between the day and night lighting, base your choices on the prevailing light when the room is used most.

Once again, the color direction was not what I had expected. Medium and lighter colors really faded away in the expanse of the room. The fabric that looked fabulous was a rosy red damask (dare I admit this…) that we liked best on the reverse side! From the beginning I had planned to use a damask in this room. I was hoping to find one with a strong central motif that we could center on the valances and perhaps outline with a trim.

The upholstered cornice board is cut to follow the outline of the crown moulding for a tight fit.

Double rows of trim outline the top and bottom edges of the cornice, while a single narrow trim traces the pattern of the central motif.

Overleaf: A view of the window and both French doors seen from one side of the room.

> **—Tip—**
>
> *Frequently, light and space in a room will dictate a color direction that is different from what you had planned. Be open and receptive to these differences. Don't be afraid to follow what your inner sense says is best.*

Solution

Our solution followed the line of my thinking with only minor changes.

Change #1. As the damask did not have a well-defined motif, I intended to "create" a motif by using a trim to outline it.

Change #2. I decided to use an upholstered cornice instead of a valance, once I saw how the fabric handled in the workroom. It wrinkled too easily and I felt, that over time, it would not hold its shape—that it would have a tendency to curl.

Change #3. The key trim was out of stock—with only half the yardage that we required available—and no stock due in for three months.

However, it turned out that this particular trim was available in two other coordinating styles. I started thinking: all three trims had a lot of yardage. But no one trim had enough yardage to be used as a single trim on the window treatment. Why not take the available yardages, work out a design, and combine the three trims to look as if I had planned it that way all along?

> **—Tip—**
>
> *Let your creativity be challenged. There is always a solution waiting to enter your life.*

All I wanted was to accomplish my goal, which was to have a really fabulous looking window treatment, and please the client. It took a bit of mathematics, but I finally arrived at a way to incorporate all three trims into an uncontrived design. It was an exhilarating challenge with fabulous results.

CASE STUDY 4

Dining Room/Parlor

Two individual rooms that work together because the same fabrics are used in different ways on the windows and doors.

In this case, a growing family, living in an old house, have an interesting combination of two rooms that are visually united by a spacious, open doorway. One room is the Dining Room and the other is used as the Front Parlor (Family Room). They want to maintain a separateness in the two rooms because the rooms are used differently.

Room and Window Review

1. A moderately-sized Dining Room and an adjoining Front Parlor, each having a window and French door.

2. Four different openings include an old original double-hung, triple window that goes to the floor; two new French doors, one in each room, used as entrances from the outside; and a casement window that probably was installed in the sixties.

3. There are differences in the space above each of the openings; differences below the openings, too.

4. Both French doors are used daily for entering and exiting.

5. This is an old farmhouse, and the ceiling line is rather uneven, but the overall height is good: 8'-10"(2.70m).

6. Each room has an old-fashioned type of radiator, rather tall. One is right up against the window in the Dining Room, and the other is too close to the French door in the Front Parlor.

Client Requests

1. They have requested that I use the same wallpaper in both rooms because of the openness between the two spaces.

2. The window treatments are pretty much up to me, but the clients want a similar feeling in the design for all of the windows.

3. I have suggested that we try rather traditional styling for the window designs, and they are quite pleased with that idea.

4. They want the window designs to be beautiful and elegant, and the fabric selections are to reflect those qualities. One of the reasons they are making this investment is because the window treatments will be included in the sale of the house, and they know that well-appointed windows will help the sale.

Design Development

The jumping off point in my thinking was to use one key fabric and develop different designs for the windows and doors. In other words, maintain the continuity of the two rooms with the same fabrics, but underscore the differences by using different designs for the window treatments.

In the Front Parlor I didn't have much trouble designing an elaborate swag and jabot arrangement, looped over a pole with some fabulous bullion fringe outlining all the lead edges for the triple window. The design was enhanced by the elegance of the long windows that extend to the floor. Scaling the swags and scarf (the straight hanging part between the swags) to work over the French door was also relatively simple. And I felt I could live with the tight space for the drapery panel hanging next to the radiator. The overall effect on both window and door designs pleased me enormously.

But when it came to the Dining Room, try as I might, I just couldn't get the same design to work on both the window and the French door.

Here the problem was the radiator. Since the radiator was located so close to the window sill, I would only be able to use fabric from the sill up. That reality was dictating the design. However, I was pretty confident that if I took the window design and put it on top of the French door, it would look good. So that is what I did.

But when I drew the window treatment over the door, I realized the design was off-balance. It was top heavy. It definitely needed something to take the eye down to the floor. A natural choice was a pair of narrow stationary panels on either side of the door opening.

Special Note: Many elements need to be considered when you're designing window treatments:

- ❀ *Heat and air conditioning sources*
- ❀ *Traffic patterns*
- ❀ *Light*
- ❀ *Activities in the space*
- ❀ *Visibility factors*
- ❀ *Personal requirements*

Color Choices: With a variety of colors in the wallpaper to choose from, I could have gone in several different directions.

The scarf and swag, draped on a fluted wood pole, are trimmed in a bullion fringe ornamented with tasseled hangers and a looped cord.

A close-up showing the detail of the bullion fringe used on the swags, scarves and jabots.

Fig. 11. French Door and Window Wall Elevation, Front Parlor.

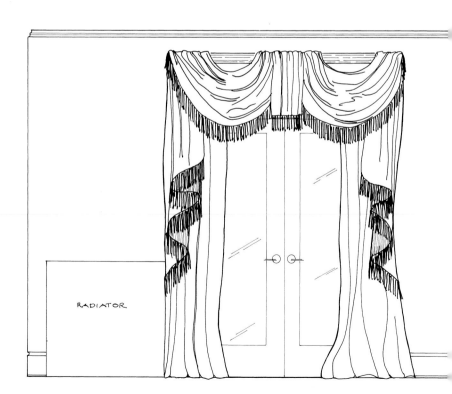

Fig. 12. A fluted wood pole holds swags, scarf and jabots over a pair of stationary drapery panels on the French door and triple window.

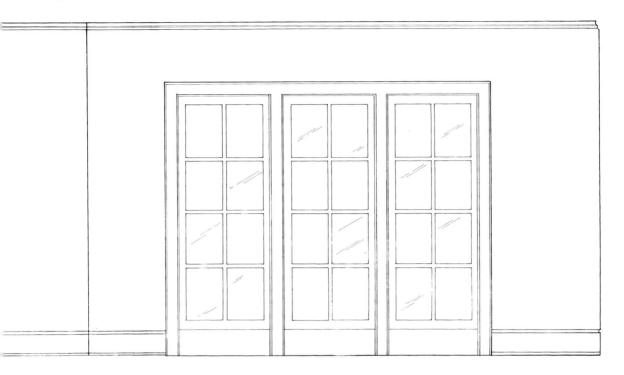

But one of the client's possessions—a beautiful red velvet sofa in the Parlor—helped me make a basic decision.

> ## —*Tip*—
>
> *Keep a personal request list. Before finalizing the design, refer back to this list to insure nothing is left out.*

I decided to use two different colors for the fabrics. One would be in the red family, and the other would be a color to work with the colors in the wallpaper. Trimming selections would come later, based on what I could find in the market.

This rather flexible approach leaves the door open to different possibilities. There is never one way to solve a design problem. There are usually several, as you will see.

With red as the key color, I went through every color family in the wallpaper—every stripe and every plaid—and couldn't find a fabric that worked. Many, many fabrics

later, I spotted a banana yellow taffeta that struck the right balance and I knew I was half way there.

One day, a red stripe fabric that had been discarded because it was too strong for the paper was still on the work table—but turned over. The reverse side of it still showed a stripe, but a tone-on-tone version with the red color much softer. It mated instantly with the banana yellow. So, here I was with a yellow and red scheme, which I had not even thought of originally. It's very interesting to see where colors will lead you, if you let them.

The same is true for trimmings. For the Parlor a beautiful combination of red, blue and yellow was available in a bullion fringe. Great. The problem was—I wanted a coordinating trim for the Dining Room. This, they did not have. Saying 'yes' to the bullion fringe, I kept looking. When I spied

> ## —*Tip*—
>
> *Follow your instincts and use whatever you think is appropriate for the particular solution.*

a gorgeous tassel fringe with a strong green in it, I reluctantly said 'yes.'

Why reluctantly? It didn't seem conventional to use a green trim in one area and blue in another, especially when the window styles were so different. The more expected choice would have been to use different fabrics with different trims. In the end, with convention safely pushed aside, I had used:

- ❀ *a fabric on the reverse side*
- ❀ *different colors in the trimmings*
- ❀ *different designs on the windows and doors*

Solution

I kept the two rooms connected by using the same fabrics on the windows and doors. I also kept the same relationships between the fabrics, which means that the

The drapery treatments installed on the window and French door incorporate two different colors in three fabrics for a bold effect.

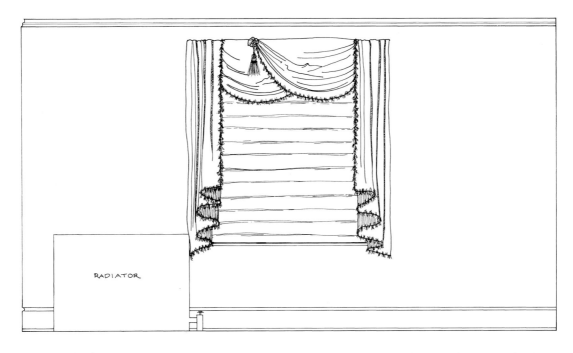

Fig. 17. On the Dining Room window, swags and jabots pose over a soft-pleated, Roman shade.

darker of the two colors was used on the upper section of the treatment and the lighter color on the lower.

The individuality of the two rooms was maintained by designing different styles for the windows and doors. The differences were intentionally accented in the color and style of the trimmings.

In the end, the window design in the Parlor has a spirited elegance to it without being too formal. It serves to underscore the purpose of the room, which is to pro-

vide a living room atmosphere in an area where friends and family come together.

In the Dining Room, the styling of the design has a more stately feel, appropriate for this room which is used primarily for sit-down dinners and buffet entertaining. ☙

Facing page: A partial view of the Dining Room window and a full-length look at the French door with their identical swags and jabots.

Insert: the tassel finishes the asymmetrically draped swag in a whimsical way.

GRAPHIC STUDY 1

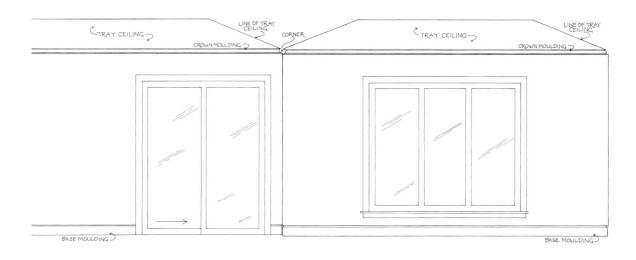

Fig. 19. Sliding Door and Window Wall Elevation, Master Bedroom.

Fig. 20. On the door and window, a formalized swag and jabot arrangement over a pair of full-length casement curtains; cords and tassels are added to complement the design.

Above: The finished installation includes a motorized blackout shade that travels up and down behind the sheer casement curtains. This shade is mounted and hidden behind the swag treatment.

Right: A detail of the bed shows the cinnamon damask which was the basis for the color selection of the fabrics in the window treatment.

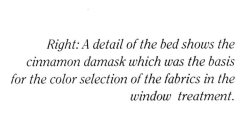

III. Easy Design Techniques for Window Treatments

Dynamic window treatments consist of styling, fabric selection and a creative solution.

ᗰCASE STUDY 5ᕲ

Front Hall

*A straightforward design that is taken out of the ordinary
by an interesting trimming technique.*

The client has asked for basic decorating in their main
rooms, as they both enjoy entertaining and want a comfortable environment for themselves and their visitors. They see
the decorating, including window treatments, as an investment. They also realize that a nicely finished interior will
make their selling job easier when they leave, since they
expect to be transferred to another region in a few years.

Room and Window Review

1. A bay window in the Entrance Hall of a house built in
   the last century, consisting of three double-hung sash
   windows.

2. The window trim is a sizable 5"(13cm) in width and
   typical of this period, meaning architecturally straightforward, rather than decorative.

3. The bay itself is rather shallow, but with a nice ceiling
   height of 106"(2.69m).

4. There is a beam running across the windows at the
   line of the original wall of the house, indicating that,
   like most bay windows, this one was added to the
   house at a later date. The net result is a difference
   between the ceiling height of the Entrance Hall and
   the small ceiling section in the bay itself.

5. The view looking onto the yard is sunny.

At close range: the double ruffle trim with its pinked edges clearly visible.

Looking toward the bay window, lightly covered with unlined balloon shades in a patterned sheer.

Fig. 21a. Bay Window Wall Elevation, Front Hall.

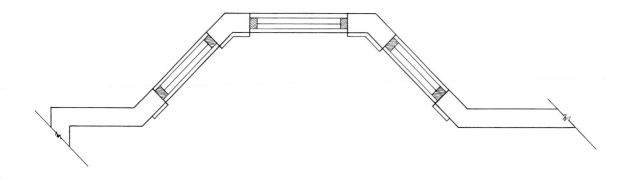

Fig. 21b. Bay window in plan.

Fig. 22. A shirred valance and a pair of stationary drapery panels frame the opening of the bay window; balloon shades cover the three windows.

Client Requests

1. This couple, with a growing family, wants an impressive entry way into their home, but not a design that would be considered grandiose.

2. Since they expect to be moving in a few years, they don't want to spend too much on this window.

3. They would like to retain as much of the view outside as possible; the wife appreciates the light that comes in during the day.

4. Other than that, they are leaving the design and the fabric and color choices to me. They wonder if I can work around the existing wallpaper and the fabric that is on the settee.

Design Development

It turned out that it was the wallpaper that gave me the direction to take. A combination of ivory and beige, the pattern is soft in coloration yet in a bold, large-scale design. While in deliberate contrast, the fabric on the settee is extremely strong—predominantly rich red and blue stripes.

I felt the way to go was using the colors of the wallpaper for the fabrics at the window and then to find trimmings to pick up the red and blue in the settee. My basic feeling was to have a window treatment that was pale. That way it would act as a frame around the entire bay opening and play up the unusual style of the settee. Once again, I wanted to use a sheer fabric at the window, unlined, for a pull-up type of shade.

Fabric Choices

A tone-on-tone stripe for the draperies and valance framing the bay was my first choice…a play on the stripe of the settee, in a color to match the wallpaper. We found a beautiful stripe that looks like two ribbons put together, one stripe is in a plain satin finish and the other has a gros-grain ribbon texture.

For the windows I wanted an old-fashioned, romantic look, but not a lace curtain feeling. I selected a modern sheer fabric with a large pattern in it—echoing the large-scale pattern of the wallpaper.

With the fabric settled, I turned to the more practical decisions that determine the styling of the window covering. In this case, I decided on balloon shades, unlined, with minimal fullness, and mechanically engineered to operate as one unit. The three individual shades would pull up as one to ensure that all three shades maintain the same level. Lastly, the question of how many 'balloons' were needed for each shade had to be settled. Usually, I prefer an odd number of balloons, but here, two balloons per shade seemed to be just right to create soft, but not overly dressed, windows.

Special Note: One of my pet peeves is to see window shades all akilter, crooked or hanging at different levels. It reflects a sloppiness that is easily corrected. If cords are broken, or other parts of a shade need replacing, take the effort to get it fixed. Or use this as the golden opportunity to take down what you have and start with something new! You will be so much happier

A shallow scallop shape to the bottom edge of the valance adds an interesting element that is enhanced by the double ruffle trim.

with windows that are finished and present a unified appearance.

I had planned to use trimmings in colors that were in the stripe fabric on the settee, but I had no luck finding anything that would work with those colors. Instead, I decided to look for a solid color fabric and use it in the form of a contrast band on the edges of the valance and draperies. And

that idea led to another—to use two colors together, treat them a little differently, and wind up with a customized effect that I wanted.

Solution

Not forgetting the beam cutting across the bay opening, I wanted a valance (or a cornice) to disguise the beam and to mask the different ceiling heights. Although I hoped to do something different with the valance, it couldn't be too complicated. I had to remember the budget.

I kept seeing 'movement' in my mind's eye for the valance. I thought if I shaped the bottom edge of the valance in some way, and then made it extra full, that would create a sense of movement. The idea of making a large scallop edge on the valance (not an expensive thing to do), and shirring the fabric, would give an unplanned look to the valance, and a feeling of movement.

The idea for the trimming actually came from someone else's windows, which I modified to suit this particular situation. I decided to use two colors in a solid fabric—beige from the wallpaper, and deep red from the stripe in the settee fabric. By layering the two together, and cutting the top layer smaller than the underneath layer, the color of the underneath fabric would peek out on both edges.

To really make it special, I decided to pink the edges of both fabrics, sew them together as one ruffled border, and attach them to the bottom edge of the valance, and the lead and bottom edges of the draperies.

This sounds more complicated than it is. In checking the finished photo on page 59, I'm sure you'll agree that this treatment lends grace and charm to the space and expresses the right degree of cordiality in the welcoming entrance of this family residence.

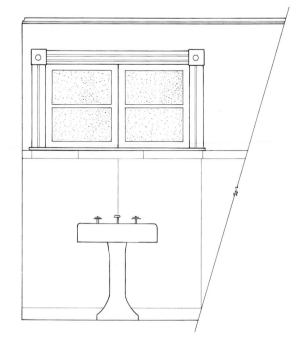

Fig. 23. Window Wall Elevation, Bathroom.

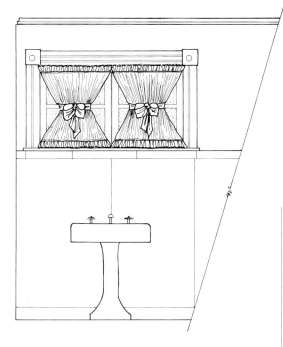

Fig. 24. A minimal window treatment, that employs practicality and charm, as well as appealing details in the trimming.

ᦤCASE STUDY 6᧤

Bathroom

A variation on an old-fashioned café curtain bridges the gap between tradition and today's definite lifestyles.

In this case, my client (the parents) had a special request for me. One of their children, unhappy with the way her Bathroom looked, asked her parents if something could be done to it. One look told me to start with the window, which indeed, needed help.

Room and Window Review

1. A bathroom belonging to a young lady (a pre-teen, to be exact); a long L-shape room on the second floor of a vintage house.

2. There are two casement windows in a wood frame, with vision-proof glass, and slide bolts at the top and bottom of the frame to hold them closed.

3. The window trim is substantial, with nice corner blocks.

4. The windows open into the room and will be used in warm weather.

Client Requests

1. Our 'client' definitely wants something pretty—in pink—to take away from the greyness of the old marble walls.

2. The parents feel that any change would be an improvement, and they have nothing specific in mind.

Design Development

Since a bathroom has a lot of moisture-related elements to consider, I knew that being able to open the windows would be a strong factor in maintaining a comfortable atmosphere. Whatever I designed for the window would have to take into account that the windows were large and swing into the room. Any window treatment that would have to be moved out of the way when someone wanted to open the windows was impractical. This being the case, the covering would have to be something that would mount directly to the window frame, be washable and pretty.

Actually, this made my decisions relatively easy, since the choices were limited.

Fabric and Color Choices

I decided to put fabric on rods, mounted top and bottom to the frame. I would use a sheer fabric and add some sort of trim to the top and bottom of the curtain. I would also make sure that everything was washable.

Although I wanted the curtain design to reflect the femininity and youthfulness of my client, I didn't want it to be overly sweet and frilly. You can probably guess what I was thinking. Yes…a plaid.

A close look at the bow and the ruffle on the bottom edge of the curtain.

The pink plaid trim really settles the issue of how a window treatment can be feminine without being overly sweet.

Combined with a sheer fabric, a plaid border would have a light, airy feeling about it.

The 'trim' or ribbon-like banding I selected was actually a plaid fabric, bubble gum pink and ivory. I chose one row of the plaid in the pattern to cut and use as a ribbon. I measured the rows in the plaid and, based on the pattern in the plaid and the width that would work best for the band, I settled on a finished measurement of 1 $\frac{5}{8}$"(4cm)

for the band. I used it in a long strip across the bottom and top edges of the fabric.

Still, I thought it needed a little something to set it off. So a band of solid pink fabric was added to provide a wee bit more contrast between the sheer curtain fabric and the plaid band. It reinforces the pink in the fabric and unifies the whole design.

Solution

The window frame needed painting and repairs. I enlisted the handiest person in the house for that—someone who could also paint the slide bolts the color of the window moulding, so they would be less noticeable on the frame.

I kept to the original idea of using a curtain shirred onto rods at the top and bottom of the window frames with one added design detail: the curtains would be tied in the center with a bow in the pink plaid fabric, trimmed with an edging of the solid pink fabric. 🌿

GRAPHIC STUDY 2

A variation of a balloon shade, the Viennese shade pictured here, in an unlined version, is an uncomplicated, elegant way to finish a window. Be sure that visibility factors are not a problem if you're going to use a shade unlined.

Graphic Study 3

Fig. 25. Window Wall Elevation, Living Room.

Fig. 26. The well-proportioned swags and jabots on these large-scale windows are designed to give the impression of a total window treatment.

Intended to work with a pair of existing balloon shades, this window treatment consists of a swag and jabots, and is impressive enough to stand on its own, without the necessity of using draperies or curtains.

GRAPHIC STUDY 4

The most stream-lined of all drapery treatments—a pair of sheer curtains that go from ceiling to floor, installed on a rod behind a minimal crown moulding, flanked by a pair of 3-panel standing screens.

At the ceiling, you see the crown moulding (a simple cove), the screen, which is very close to ceiling height, and the curtains, softly shirred.

IV. DRESSING THE WINDOW FOR PRIVACY OR CLIMATE CONTROL

How to create creature comfort and attractive window treatments that work together.

ᒐᘓCASE STUDY 7ᘐᒑ

Bedroom

Styled for privacy and air flow, this window treatment presents an exciting, yet unusually simple solution in the design.

Here is a case of a one-bedroom rental apartment with a new tenant who asked me to create a lovely, liveable Bedroom, suited to her blossoming lifestyle.

Room and Window Review

1. The Bedroom is in an apartment on the second floor of an historic building that has been converted for residential use.

2. There is only one window, a typical double-hung sash style, with absolutely no view. Any original moulding is long gone.

3. It faces a brick wall, with windows of other apartments in plain sight. Very little light coming in.

4. The window is actually set into a recess of 6 ½" (16.5cm) in the wall; the ceiling height is good: 8'–10" (2.69m).

Client Requests

1. Not worried about the lack of a view; wants a pretty, but not fussy, window treatment.

2. Wants to be able to block out the brick wall, control her visibility in the room, yet maintain air circulation.

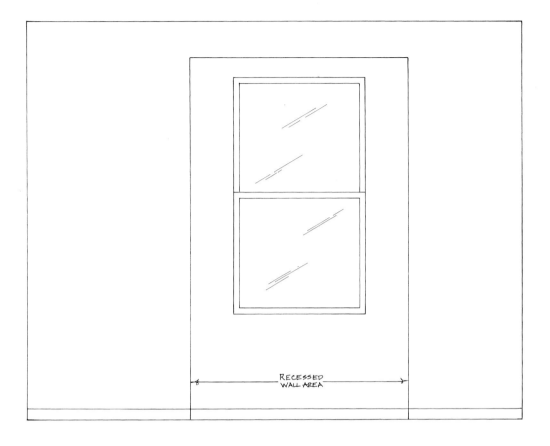

RECESSED
WALL AREA

Fig. 27. Window Wall Elevation, Bedroom.

3. She wants the finished treatment to be easily maintained.

4. Most important of all—how much is it going to cost?

Design Development

In what I think is pretty typical for today's young professionals, this woman had purchased a pair of curtains from a mail order catalogue and had hung them herself.

Even though she had done little else to the room, it was evident that she cared about her space and was ready to take on certain projects by herself. Basically, she wanted a design for the entire room—her budget wouldn't allow her to go beyond that for the moment.

We agreed that the design would be simple enough for her to execute herself, as

Fig. 28. The design for this window has a cornice board at the ceiling with a pair of casement curtains and stationary drapery panels installed behind it.

she was planning on doing the sewing! Staying with a simple, straightforward style for the window and bed coverings, I felt we needed an unusual color or fabric to bring it to life.

What could be simpler than a classic casement curtain in front of the window, and in front of that, a pair of straight hanging, stationary drapery panels? Styled with a large border on the lead edges and along the bottom that would give the windows a distinctive look, we could take the whole treatment up to the ceiling, and successfully eliminate the unsightly recess around the window itself.

In formulating my thinking about how the treatment would finish at the ceiling, I made the connection between the 'large'

The wallpaper border serves as a crown moulding and finishes the cornice.

The principal paisley pattern and the related fabrics used in the scheme.

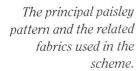

A nice detail is the hem in the casements that matches the border on the draperies.

border on the draperies and the idea of a cornice board, which could be very easily constructed and installed in front of the window treatment. How to finish the cornice was still a question: paint (boring) or fabric (maybe, but then the cornice should be upholstered for it to look right; could my client handle that part?).

One day, I was looking through a book of wallpaper borders for a totally different project, and I came upon an interesting border that was a little over 6"(16cm) high. I knew that putting up a border around the perimeter of her room was a task that my client could handle herself.

Moreover, it was a very affordable solution, and would really give the room a definite design element that it very much needed. By making the border on the draperies the same width as the wallpaper

╭─────────────────────────────╮
│ ──*Tip*── │
│ │
│ *Don't 'force' a design. Let* │
│ *the creative elements in* │
│ *your imagination unfold* │
│ *and produce a design that* │
│ *naturally flows together* │
│ *out of the various ele-* │
│ *ments of your project.* │
╰─────────────────────────────╯

border, we would introduce a nice professional detail in the room. And that's how the drapery treatment that you see on the facing page came to be.

Special Note: When you are looking for something, be receptive to the fact that you don't know at what exact moment that 'something' is going to materialize in front of you.

Fabric Choices

I wanted to use a cotton fabric, a contemporary chintz pattern, for this client, something as bright and cheery as she is. A group of new prints caught my eye one day, and I found the perfect pattern, a contemporary interpretation of a traditional paisley motif—in a palette of intense colors that were truly exciting.

I felt the casement curtain fabric should visually eliminate the unattractive brick wall outside. It should be sheer to the eye, but should be able to mask the brick wall. We selected a woven check pattern in a creamy color for the curtains or 'sheers', as they are frequently called.

The fabric we selected for the border is totally opposite in feeling from the paisley motif of the drapery fabric. It creates an

The full-length draperies and casement curtains visually increase the height of the room and provide the focal point as well.

—*Tip*—

Be warned—no drapery treatment will ever look right, hang right or feel right if it is not lined. It will look even better if it is interlined. (For a definitive statement on interlining, see page 92 of this book).

interesting tension—always a necessary element in making any room successful.

Solution

One of my goals in this project was to keep the installation as simple as possible, since my 'installer' was going to be the client herself. To this end, I said: Let's use casement curtains shirred onto a rod for the sheers. By doing this, we eliminated the need to install a traverse rod.

For the times she wants to open the window, I provided narrow, self-fabric tiebacks. One is attached to the wall at either side of the window, where it is hidden behind the curtains. She can pull the fabric back from the window, hook the tie

around it and still maintain a soft, pretty look at the window.

To give the client total control over her privacy, I decided to reuse the mini blinds on the window (inherited from the previous tenant). They would not be visible behind the casements and would be a definite cost-saving feature in the budget.

Final word here: The solution for this particular window is simple enough for someone with average sewing skills to execute. The reason it looks great is because the window treatment was carefully thought out. The dynamic fabric for the draperies creates an important element in the room. Since the client was so enthusiastic about wanting to use more of it, we reinforced its importance by deciding to use it for the dust ruffle.

—Tip—

Be sensitive to the light, the direction the window faces and the view outside. All contribute to the design of a window treatment.

☙CASE STUDY 8❧

Dressing Area

A deceptively easy idea, a window shade of fabric provides coverage, sun control and a strong design statement.

A small Bedroom with one double window and a single window presented a unique design challenge: how to provide both solar protection and privacy. Both are big design issues today. This case study focuses on the treatment for the single window.

Room and Window Review

1. A single, double-hung window in the dressing area at one end of a bedroom.
2. An unobstructed East view, facing buildings and other apartments.
3. The client is very visible from the outside.
4. There is lots of morning sun.
5. The recently reconstructed closets have new doors.

Client Requests

1. As the client's wardrobe is very important to her, she wants it fully protected from the sun.

2. It goes without saying that she does not want to be seen by the neighbors when she is dressing.

3. If possible, she would like the treatment for this window to look like the treatment on the principal window in the room shown on page 26.

Design Development

Because of the way the closet doors and small cabinet were built in their relationship to the window, there was no way to develop a window treatment that would resemble the one I was designing for the large window in the room. Actually, there didn't seem to be any room at all to hang fabric. I shifted my attention to the problem of her visibility in this area and protecting her wardrobe.

It was clear that with all the morning sun streaming in, we needed a sunproof shading device to protect the clothing and control the build-up of heat. The closet doors helped block the light, but only when they were closed.

The idea of using a shade in one of the sunproof types of material that would be hanging next to the wall upholstery didn't thrill me at all. You see, the client and I

A view in the dressing area of the Roman shade on the window, the wall upholstery and cabinetry.

Here you see the superb matching of the shade fabric with the fabric on the walls.

had already decided to upholster the bedroom walls with fabric. Sometimes it takes awhile to see the obvious.

What was the obvious? Take the wall upholstery fabric and use it for the shade. Eureka! I loved the idea of this extravagant bold pattern continuing around the room, and across the window.

In order to maintain the pattern undistorted by folds, pleats or shirring, a straight hanging Roman shade was the really the best choice of shade. When a Roman shade is fully extended, covering the window, it is simply a straight run of fabric. I had to make sure that the pattern in the fabric for the shade absolutely lined up with, and matched, the fabric on the walls surrounding the window.

This is not as difficult as it sounds. I had to make sure to have enough fabric for matching the pattern (or use a fabric that doesn't have a pattern), and work carefully with the wall upholsterer and the shade fabricator (frequently, they are the same person). This way the shade becomes part of the room's wall upholstery and does not infringe on the design of the other window. Look at the fabulous results in the photographs on the facing page.

ᗙ CASE STUDY 9 ᗙ

Master Bedroom

Window shades and draperies combine to make one wall into a luxurious statement that provides the design for a room.

These clients had only recently moved into this apartment when we were introduced. For budgetary reasons they wanted to approach the decorating on a room-by-room basis. Their Bedroom, a very ordinary space, was my first assignment. I thought we should start with the windows.

Room and Window Review

1. A one-room addition to an early 20th century residence, probably built in the sixties, now being used as the Master Bedroom.

2. Typical of the construction of the sixties, this is a perfectly plain space, no mouldings in the room—not even trim around the windows; the ceiling height is not bad: 8'–10"(2.70m).

3. There are two windows, off-center, on the wall overlooking a garden in the rear of the building; northern exposure.

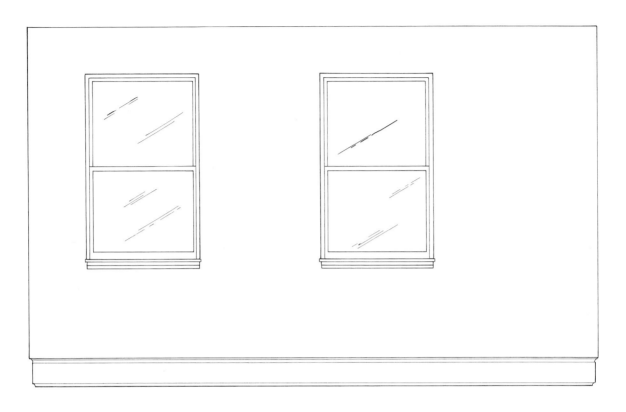

Fig. 29. Window Wall Elevation, Master Bedroom.

4. The windows are short with an unusu-ally high sill; the space above the win-dows is adequate, 14"(36cm).

Client Requests

1. Since the room is so plain, this couple wants a really handsome window treat-ment. They expect it to be the domi-nant element in the room, even more so than the bed treatment.

2. They are very tight on space in this room and are emphatic about not hav-ing the drapery treatment take up pre-cious inches.

3. As far as style is concerned, they express a desire for a certain formality in the design.

4. They have a nice view and whatever I put on the windows should be able to be moved aside to maintain the view.

5. There are white black-out roller shades on the windows now; the client needs

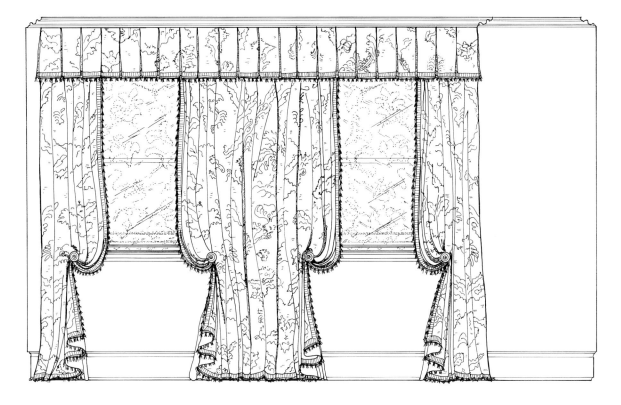

Fig. 30. Crown moulding is added to provide an architectural element behind which a pleated valance and stationary drapery panels are installed; Roman shades fit within the window opening.

coverage more from the standpoint of privacy, than from the morning light, since these windows face North.

Design Development

Frequently, the real story of the windows and their relationship to everything else on the wall is told in the drawing of the wall elevation. In this case, I had a basic, bare-bones outline in my head of how I thought this window should look.

But when I looked at the elevation, after it was drawn, I had to revise my thinking. If you look at the elevation as shown on the facing page you will see the spacing of the windows on the wall is quite off-center. There is not adequate space between the windows for using separate drapery panels on each window.

Several decisions were made quickly, based on the information revealed in the elevation. Specifically:

1. we need a crown moulding at the ceiling;

2. the two windows will be joined by a single drapery panel designed to bridge the space between the two windows;

3. a strong floor-to-ceiling treatment will downplay the imbalance of the window location on the wall.

The windows are not wide. In order to preserve any of the view outside, I had to keep the fabric off the glass area as much as possible. It occurred to me to use the old-fashioned decorative metal tiebacks, where the fabric is simply pulled back over short rods that are fastened into the wall. The decorative rosette on the metal tieback would also bring in a note of formality.

Fabric and Color Choices

I knew this treatment would need a strong trimming to outline and emphasize the design, and a bold pattern in a special fabric—neither too feminine nor too masculine—to make a maximum statement. Perhaps a plaid or a classical chintz pattern… But not for this client, it turned out. They related to more sophisticated designs. And guess who found it?

It was one of those instances where the instincts of the client, in this case the husband, were right on target. The husband selected something that is so perfect for the room that I had to admire his choice and his ability to follow his instincts. The fabric, which you see in close-up on the facing page, is a mix of deep, rich claret colors in a large traditional damask motif, printed on a honey-colored ground. It is soft and elegant, like a man's silk robe. Perfection.

Facing page: The drapery fabric.

Top inset: The crown moulding forms a pocket inside where the mechanics of the window treatment are located.

Bottom inset: The layers of trim, the brass tieback and sheer fabric of the shade seen in detail.

Double-page spread: The coordinating lining in a shade of honey peeks out from the drapery at the window—one of several details that gives this window treatment an elegant quality.

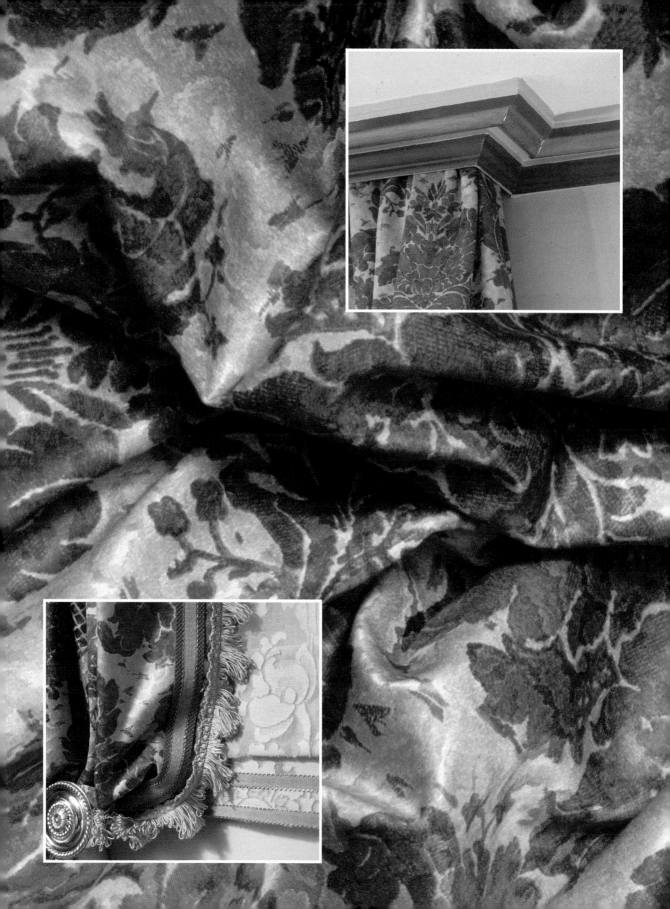

For the windows themselves, I thought of using an unlined sheer fabric for pleated pull-up Roman shades and keeping the clients' black-out roller shades behind them. The reason my thinking went in the direction of using a fabric shade, as opposed to thinking of a floor length casement curtain, was because of the clients' request to keep this treatment as close to the wall as possible. Eliminating the layer of a curtain will save us 3"–4"(8-10cm) in the floor space of the room.

Solution

In every solution there are shifts in direction that change and modify the original design. These shifts occur for many different reasons.

* *Sometimes a fabric or trim is out of stock at the last moment, forcing a hasty substitution, as happened here with one of the trims.*

* *Sometimes an element will catch your eye and create an opportunity to improve the design, as happened here with the two fabrics.*

* *Every once in awhile, you have to admit that what you are looking for simply doesn't exist, as was the case with one of the trims.*

As I noted earlier, I saw the trim as a very important ingredient in the design. But I just couldn't find any trim in a color that would work with the fabric.

—Tip—

Remember that things always work out for the best. Don't force decisions. Let changes in the design process work for you.

So I decided to do what comes naturally: layer. I would find colors in trims that I could layer, one on top of the other or in combination, so that when they were sewn together on the drapery, they would look like one beautiful trim.

What may look like a single trim on the edges of the valance and draperies, is actually three trims used in combination:

* *a loop fringe, scallop edge, honey beige color, applied to the outermost edge of the fabric*

* *a woven flat braid, basketweave texture, in a claret color, set in from the edge*

❋ *a narrow grosgrain ribbon with a picot edge, honey beige color, placed on top of the wider claret color braid*

When I was in the workroom reviewing the fabrics, I discovered that the motif in the sheer fabric for the Roman shades was almost identical to the motif in the drapery fabric.

I decided to align the motif of the shade with the motif of the fabric in the valance.

That meant restyling the valance. The new version (as compared to the original version in the drawing on page 81) now has a flat section the size of the motif. The motif is centered on the valance and over each window, with shirred sections in between.

Now, when I look at this beautiful window treatment that the client is so thrilled with, I am grateful for the things that didn't go right.

GRAPHIC STUDY 5

A Powder Room, facing the front yard, where a Viennese shade—easily pulled up or down—gives the visitor complete control over personal privacy requirements. A tone-on-tone cotton stripe fabric is quietly trimmed with a matching moss fringe on the bottom edge of the shade.

GRAPHIC STUDY 6

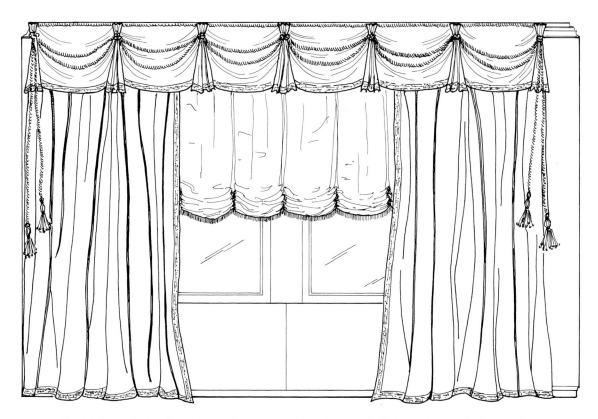

Fig. 31. The window in a Master Bedroom, with cabinetry built in underneath the window to completely conceal the HVAC system inside. Unseen, behind the balloon shade, is a blackout roller shade installed on each window, pulled down every night for light and privacy requirements on the part of occupants.

Facing page: The finished installation shows cords swagged over the valance and knotted at each trumpet, ending in long lengths of cord with tassels that trail down the side of the draw draperies. These draperies are designed to close in front of the balloon shade, or as you see in the photograph, look very handsome in a partially open position.

GUIDELINES FOR CREATING A WINDOW TREATMENT

1. To begin, look at the window and wall as being architectural elements. Understand the basic shapes and proportions: rectangle, square, vertical or horizontal.

2. Consider the window opening as an integral part of the entire wall elevation, not as an isolated element.

3. It will be necessary to draw the entire wall on paper, as best you can. If you can't do this in the form of a scaled drawing, find someone who can and pay them for this service.

4. Do not sketch what you think you would like to have, or think you should have for a window treatment **before** having the full window elevation to look at.

5. Look at the window. Take into consideration the direction the window faces and the light that comes in.

6. Will the furnishings and fabrics in the room need protection from strong daylight or direct sun?

7. Does the comfort level of the room occupant require controlling heat and/or cold factors that are directly related to the window?

8. Describe the activities that take place in the room. List only the most important ones.

9. Does daylight contribute in any way, whether negatively or positively, to these activities?

10. With regard to personal privacy, is the window treatment to provide a lot of coverage, minimal coverage or something in between?

FABRIC

GROUP A

Qualities

Sheer or lightweight; soft, supple, silky, open weaves; soft, fluid draping qualities: fair to good results; sheer, translucent, not light-blocking, even when lined.

Fibers

Synthetic fibers, or combinations of synthetic and natural fibers; cotton, silk, sheer wool, lightweight linen.

Uses

Casement curtains, draperies, swags and/or jabots, valances, cornices, unlined shades. Can be self-lined or lined with another sheer or other lightweight fabric.

11. Will the treatment consist of one fabric, a combination of different layers of fabrics and/or light controlling devices?

12. Focus on the visibility and privacy factors:

a. Is there a view? Good___ Nondescript___ Awful___

b. Is there a reason to focus attention on the view?

c. Is there a reason to ignore the view?

d. Does the occupant mind being visible? Only at night___ All the time___ Doesn't mind___

CHART — QUALITIES AND USES

GROUP B

Qualities

Light or medium weight; soft, crisp, silky, textured weaves; soft, fluid, good body in draping qualities: good to excellent results; translucent, opaque, can be light-blocking.

Fibers

Cotton, silk, wool, linen; synthetic fibers. Combinations of synthetic and natural fibers; combinations of natural fibers.

Uses

Curtains, draperies, swags/jabots, valances, cornices, shades. For lining use regular (cotton sateen), thermal, or black-out lining; or a contrast lining (any fabric in a different color or pattern). Can take light to medium weight interlining.

GROUP C

Qualities

Medium to heavyweight; supple, soft, crisp, textural, dimensional; good to excellent draping qualities: excellent results; opaque, usually light-blocking.

Fibers

Cotton, silk, wool, linen; synthetic fibers; combinations of synthetic and natural fibers; combinations of natural fibers.

Uses

Draperies, swags/jabots, valances, cornices, shades. For lining use regular (cotton sateen), thermal, or black-out lining; or a contrast lining (any fabric of a different color or pattern). Can take medium to heavy-weight interlining.

e. Does the occupant want to be able to see out? All or most of the time___ Infrequently___ Doesn't care___

f. Does the occupant want to see out and have light coming in, but not be visible to others?

g. Is there a need to be able to control the amount of light that comes in and when it comes in?

The answers to questions 1 – 12 will help you determine the number of layers in the treatment that you will need, as well as the different kinds of drapery hardware that will be required to install it. This is information that you need, whether you are doing your own design and installation, or whether someone else will be doing it for you. Additionally, the following issues must be considered:

13. Are there any special requirements on the part of the occupant that need to be taken into account?

14a. What is the period or style of the residence (or room) where the window is located?

14b. Is the style of the window treatment to reflect the period or style of the room?

14c. Or is it to be a counterpoint to the general feeling of the space?

14d. A note of caution: creating a design that is supposed to make a point, just because it is 'different,' is destined to flop. A window treatment is not designed to take over a room. Yes, it can be, and often is, the focal point and dominant element in a space. But always the effect should be to enhance the interior and invite the visitor in. This is best achieved by keeping the design in harmony with the overall style of the room. To make a specific statement, try using a special fabric and/or color scheme.

15. What kind, or combination, of fabrics would you like to have on the window? Look at the suggestions in the fabric chart on pages 90 – 91 for guidance in selecting a particular fabric direction. Then give some thought to using an interlining, based on the following reasons.

Special Note on Interlining:

It is the use of an interlining in combination with a lining that makes a drapery treatment look elegant and finished. It provides a weight and dimension to the treatment that is noticeable, even to the unpracticed eye.

Almost any fabric will drape better with an interlining. The exceptions are lightweight cottons and linens, and fabrics that have a lot of body, meaning a stiffness or crispness to them. Then an interlining will add even more weight to the fabric, which, in such a case, you wouldn't want.

The unsuspected bonus in using an interlining is its thermal quality. It is an important element in blocking ventilation at a window and is frequently used just for this purpose.

Is there an added expense in the use of interlining? Yes, because of the cost of the material and the labor involved. But an interlining more than pays for itself by extending the life of your drapery treatment, lowering your heating and/or cooling bills, and giving you an exceptionally luxurious feeling to the window treatment.

16. Now you are ready to start the design. Think of all the things you want the window treatment to do. Think of how much it is to cover—or leave exposed. What styles will accomodate such diverse elements as shielding sunlight, blocking a view, providing coverage at night, letting light in or masking an imperfect condition?

Your responses start the creative wheels turning and ideas begin to formulate… perhaps a swag; maybe something long, to the floor; why not draperies that draw? At this point, make sure you have some tracing paper on hand (any art supply store will have it). Place a piece of it over the elevation of your window. You can draw on the tracing paper, yet still see the outline of the window underneath. Now take a pencil, and make a line where you think you'd like to see some fabric.

17. Once the design is underway, start to focus on colors, fabric and trimming selections.

18. Finally, consider the budget.

When you have installed a beautifully designed and detailed window treatment in a room, you have added an element of constant joy and comfort to your life. You have also added your point of view regarding the design and style of the window treatment and the room. These are all qualities for which a price tag has little merit. But for years to come, you will continue to enjoy the pleasure that this investment in a window treatment has brought. 🌿

Make a line:

For more coverage:

Draw a few more lines:

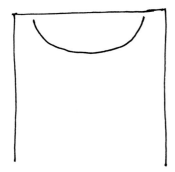

For a larger window:

Add some more lines with a few wiggles:

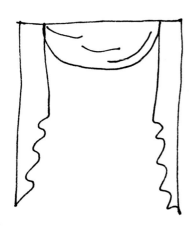

❧CREDITS☙

(Listed in alphabetical order.)

Agostino Antiques, Ltd.
Antique furniture, reproductions and accessories. Front cover, pgs. 3, 9, 26, 31, 38-39, 47

Beatrice Designs, Inc.
Decorative home accessories. Pg. 11

Bebe Winkler Interior Design, Inc.
Photography. Pgs. 51, 53, 64, 66, 87, 89

Boussac of France, Inc.
Fabrics. Pgs. 9, 25, 26, 28, 73, 75, 78

Century Furniture
Upholstered furniture, tables, accessories. Pg. 11

Decorators Walk
Furniture, decorative accessories. Front cover, pgs. 3, 16, 31, 38, 47, 49, 69, 84

Dominic Castellanos,
Painting and papering. Pg. 67

France Voiles Company, Inc.
Sheer fabrics. Pgs. 9, 26, 67, 73, 75

F. Schumacher & Co.
Fabrics, trimmings. Pg. 67

Interiors by Robert
Drapery and upholstery fabrications. Front cover, pgs. 3, 9, 11, 25, 26, 28, 31, 37, 38-39, 43, 47, 49, 55, 59, 62, 63, 67, 69, 78, 83, 84-85

John Boone, Inc.
Accessories, tables. Pg. 67

Julia Gray Ltd.
Antique and reproduction furniture, accessories. Pgs. 47, 49

Lewis Mittman, Inc.
Manufacturers of custom furniture. Pg. 11

MBL Contracting Corp.
General contractors and architectural woodworking. Pg. 78

Saxony Carpet Company, Inc.
Carpeting and area rugs. Pgs. 9, 28, 78

Scalamandré Inc.
Fabrics, trimmings and wallpaper borders. Front cover, pgs. 3, 31, 37, 38-39, 43, 47, 49, 55, 59, 62, 63, 69, 73, 75, 83, 84-85

Scott Eberman
Electrical work. Pg. 78

Simply Country, Wilton, Connecticut
Antique accessories. Pg. 75

Standard Trimming Company
Trimmings. Pgs. 11, 43, 47, 49

Stroheim & Romann, Inc.
Fabrics and trimmings. Endpapers.

Victor Carl Antiques
Antique light fixtures and accessories. Pg. 49

Waverly
Fabrics and wallpaper borders. Pg. 11

Yale R. Burge Antiques, Inc.
Antique furniture and accessories, reproductions. Front cover, pgs. 3, 11, 38-39, 47, 55, 59, 69, 83, 84-85

ACKNOWLEDGEMENTS

It would be impossible to imagine this series of books on decorating being written without the cooperation, kindness and genuine desire to help that so many, many people in the Interior Design industry have extended to me. I wish there were room to thank each and everyone of you individually, but for now I shall confine myself as follows:

For always being available and graciously offering whatever I seemed to need at the moment, I am truly indebted to:

> *The staff in the New York showroom and at the mill of Scalamandré Inc.; the entire staff at Interiors by Robert; the staff at Yale R. Burge Antiques; the staff at the New York showroom of Century Furniture; the staff in the New York showroom of Boussac of France; and the staff at Agostino Antiques, New York City.*

For providing advice, back-up support, and professional guidance, I would like to specially thank:

> *Giselle Barreau-Freeman; Bob and Katie Bitter; Robert Boccard; Frank and Lenore Koe; Kirk Phillips; Joan Rice; and Bebe Winkler, ASID.*

But most of all, I would like to acknowledge the love and single-minded conviction of my parents, Dr. Stuart Grayson, and my dear friend, Ellen L. Vanook.